# Family Spell

## How to Break Free from a Controlling Family

## Debra Jo Hope

# Family Spell

*How to Break Free from a Controlling Family*
February 2018

Copyright © Debra Joe Hope

All rights reserved. Printed in the United States of America. No part of this publication may be reproduced, stored in a retrieval system, or transmitted, in any form or by any means electronic, mechanical, photocopying, recording, or otherwise, without the prior written permission of the author.

Unless otherwise noted, all Scripture quotations are from the English Standard Version ® (ESV®), copyright © 2001 by Crossway, a publishing ministry of Good Publishers. Used by permission. All rights reserved.

Extensive quotes from the book, Discernment, are by the author's expressed permission.
Discernment, Charles Pretlow © May 2013
ISBN 978-0-9801768-4-1

Family Spell
ISBN 978-1-943412-23-5

Published by –
Wilderness Voice Publishing
Canon City, Colorado USA
www.wvpbooks.com

"A voice crying in the wilderness -
proclaiming the good news of the coming Kingdom!"

## Christ on breaking the Family Spell

*"Do not think that I came to bring peace on the earth; I did not come to bring peace, but a sword. For I came to set a man against his father, and a daughter against her mother, and a daughter-in-law against her mother-in-law; and a man's enemies will be the members of his household. He who loves father or mother more than Me is not worthy of Me; and he who loves son or daughter more than Me is not worthy of Me"* (Matthew 10:34–37 NASB).

This message if for the mature Christian only . . .
*"But solid food is for the mature, whom because of practice have their senses trained to discern good and evil"* (Hebrews 5:14 NASB).

"You'll be there between each line of pain and glory . . ." [1]

In my case, Jesus was my biggest helper in this whole experience, so thank You, Lord. You are good all the time!

---

[1] Gladys Knight and the Pips, "Best thing That Ever Happened to Me."

# Contents

1. Family of Control — 5
2. Tolerating Evil — 8
3. The Control Continues — 10
4. Threats and Lies — 12
5. The Confrontation — 14
6. False Guilt — 19
7. The Vindication — 21
8. It's a New Day — 25
Prayer for Dealing with Controlling Relatives — 34

## Chapter 1
# Family of Control

*"I appeal to you brothers, to watch out for those who cause divisions and create obstacles contrary to the doctrine that you have been taught . . . by smooth talk and flattery they deceive the hearts of the naïve."*
Romans 16:17–18

Sitting in the Georgia sunshine, I listened to the birds singing and the water splashing onto the beach as I moved my toes slowly through the sand. On this beautiful day, a new beginning was slowly emerging as a butterfly came out of a cocoon. This was much the same as my new life. After many decades, I had finally broken free—free from a life of being controlled and manipulated. For such a long time, I thought I would never see this day, thought I would never breathe in life again, like inhaling the scent of a beautiful flower. As I relaxed, my mind went back to one of my earliest memories and how it all began.

At the age of four, my life was so very simple. I had long hair, and it needed to be brushed out every day, generally by my mother. But on this day, she was busy, so she asked my older sister to do it. My mother went into her bedroom and closed the door, unable to hear what was happening in the living room. And my sister brushed my hair, pulling and tugging on it and calling me upsetting names. The more I asked her to stop, the more she seemed to enjoy the fact that she was actually hurting me.

After the brushing was completed, my mother came out of the bedroom and asked how I was doing. Quickly answering for me, my sister said, "Oh she's doing great," and commented on what a "wonderful job" she had done. My mother agreed that my sister had done a wonderful job and my sister giggled in delight. She had fooled my mom again. Little did I know this behavior and pulling the wool over my mother's eyes would continue throughout her whole life.

The truth was, my sister, as many people told me over the years, was very jealous of my arrival on the scene, which happened when she was a teenager. Having been the "queen of the castle" and an only child all those years, her reign ended upon my birth. But she was bound and determined to have control of the house again. Because she was so good at hiding her evil deeds, she fooled a lot of people—mostly my mother—and whenever she didn't get enough attention, her anger flared. My mother, being a rather quiet person, had no idea how to discipline her. Instead of scolding her, so as to not have to deal with her rage, my mother let her "get away with murder" time and time again.

A few years later, my sister got married and ended up living, of all places, in the house right next door to my mother and father—and me. She proceeded to have children, and we often heard her screaming loudly at them, using foul language, calling them names, and blaming them for her life's problems. And so, the rage continued.

I had been raised in a very traditional and strict "religious" church and home. My family's nationality carried with it many rules, which you didn't dare go against. As it happened, I became a born-again Christian while in my teens, and this greatly disturbed my family, and my sister in particular. Years later, I got married to a man who was also a born-again Christian, which further aggravated them all. Little did we know on our wedding day how much we would end up being hated by my family as the years went on.

## Chapter 2
# Tolerating Evil

*And lead us not into temptation, but deliver us from evil."* Matthew 6:13

As my married life continued, I excelled in my career, often getting written about in local newspapers. Since I was living close to my family of origin, they would read these articles and also hear of the work we were doing in our church. My sister would make sarcastic quips at our family's holiday gatherings about how "some people here are respected and holier-than-thou," even though we never forced our beliefs on my family in any way. These comments continued for years and we sat there and said nothing.

One year, however, after the holiday dinner was completed, my sister insisted that I do a particular task to help, and she became very obnoxious about it. It wasn't that I was unwilling to help, but her demanding ways were—to put it mildly—mean and uncalled for. So after her raging at me in front of my family about how I "wasn't being at all helpful," I spoke to her quietly but firmly, saying, among other things, that she was "not my boss." That put her into such a rage that there are no words to describe it, and she ran like a child would to tell my mother. Not wanting to deal with her anger again, my mother told me to go and apologize to my sister! So, to "keep the peace" in the family, I apologized, and "all was well" again with my sister. She had gotten attention because of her screaming fit and had gotten her way again. Her husband and children, by the way, gave in to her every demand, as they were also afraid of her anger.

These screaming fits of my sister's went on for years after this. Whoever did not give in to her would be the recipient of one of her vicious rages. She even had a sign posted in her home that read, "If mama doesn't get her way, all will pay." She was taking the reins of the lives of all around her.

## Chapter 3
# The Control Continues

*"But the fruit of the Spirit is love, joy, peace, patience, kindness, goodness, faithfulness, gentleness, and self-control."* Galatians 5:22–23 NASB

My sister's rages continued but took on a new demonic energy when my father left my mother for another woman years later. At that time, my sister stormed into my mother's home, declaring loudly that she was now the head of the family and my mother was to be in strict submission to her! My sister claimed she was "loving and protecting" my mom by every decision she now made for her, and my mom rarely ever expressed her opinion. My sister's plan seemed to be to also get my husband and me out of the family so as to have full control of my mother in every way.

This entire issue was a huge spiritual battle. My sister continually interfered with my husband's and my attempts to get my mother to forgive my father (though we never agreed with his actions). When someone eventually led my mother to the Lord, my sister was quite upset, even though she and her husband said, at this point, that they had "been saved." But they were in an extremely liberal church that was often fooled by my sister's "giving spirit," and rarely saw the side of her that we did. She kept this part of herself very carefully hidden. This church actually contributed to her controlling ways, as there was no discipline there; so she even had the church on her side now.

## Chapter 4
# Threats and Lies

*"You will know them by their fruits."*
                              Matthew 7:16 NASB

Fast-forwarding to many years later now, my mother's health was beginning to fail and my sister insisted that my mother live with her and her husband, though we knew this would allow my sister even more control over her. My mother used to often comment to us, "God forbid I should live with her. Pray for me—you know how she is." When we suggested a good nursing home, my sister accused us of "trying to abandon her." As it was not possible for my husband and me to take her into our home, since we were both working full time, we succumbed to the plan. And so my mother made the move to my sister's home.

At this point, my husband and I went to see her twice a week, and my sister would call often and tell us to "be here now" to help, with no warning. Again, to "keep the peace," we would stop everything and go. If we refused, my sister would hang up on us and tell people we didn't love my mother. She used many of these incidents to make her look like the loving, giving sister, gaining attention and compliments from those around her. We were in a double-bind situation: if we helped, my sister would still tell people we didn't do enough to help, and if we couldn't help with her last-minute requests, we were hung up on and spoken against.

The battle raged on.

## Chapter 5
# The Confrontation

*"For they exchanged the truth of God for a lie. . . . And just as they did not see fit to acknowledge God any longer, God gave them over to a depraved mind, to do those things which are not proper."*
*Romans 1:25-28 NASB*

Charles Pretlow's book on discernment states: "The discerning saint who desires to set proper boundaries will virtually be on their own—however, Christ will always be on the side of the sincere; He will never leave or forsake those who are seriously learning to obey Him. . . . Sooner than later, a blowup will occur if the sincere Christian stays true to Christ. . . . Often the true saint will end up looking like they are off, unloving, or in some kind of a cult."[2]

And this is exactly what ended up happening to my husband and me.

The health of my mother was growing increasingly worse, and she was in the hospital one day when my sister, who was at the hospital

---

[2] Charles Pretlow, *Discernment*, Wilderness Voice Publishing, Canon City, CO, pp 309

with her, called us to come. As usual, we went as called. When we entered my mother's room, my mother greeted us with, "So why do you not love me?" How my sister had brainwashed her! This question was especially strange because if we didn't love her, we wouldn't be there to help. And then began a thirty-five-minute rant from my sister, falsely accusing us of not being there to help over the last few months. We had responded to all of her last-minute phone calls, mind you, except for two times when we had emergency situations. But we just had not done enough to help in the exact way she had wanted. My sister told us not to come and see my mother again, and there were many threats and swear words attached to those threats. She told us many times to "burn in hell," as my mother just sat there and, as usual, did not correct her. As we were barely able to get in any words throughout this ordeal, we got up and started to leave. My sister insisted we give her back her house key so we could not "sneak back into the house" to see my mother.

At this point I asked, "Are you sure this is the way you want this situation to be?"

She responded emphatically, "Oh yes!"

As we left the building, we were hearing the Lord say to us, "Do you love me more than these?" That was quite the question, as we were being severely tested. We felt we had a choice between following the Lord or forsaking his ways to be more acceptable to my sister.

Within a short period of time, we became aware that the vast majority of the family was taking the side of my sister, not even allowing us to present our side of the story when we would encounter them. People were being told that we didn't love my mother and were not there to help. E-mails and letters had been written and sent out about the situation to brainwash anyone who would listen. Because of fear of my sister's wrath, people would agree with her. "Groupthink" or "pack mentality" mentality is powerful as people tend to side with the more forceful of the personalities in cases like this because of fear.

This type of pack mentality went on for years in our family and community, and we ended up traveling for months at a time and eventually moving away to escape this wrath. We were being shunned by the whole family, which is all part of the "game playing" of an immature Christian's life.

Enlisting the aid of Christian counselors, we tried to endure the lonely walk of being lied about, which went on and on. In the process of all this, we wrote my mother several letters, telling her we were sorry if she felt we were not there enough to help. We told her this was not true, and that we would not be controlled by the family's thoughts and actions. We later found out from many sources that my mother was never allowed to see any of those letters, or any of the cards or gifts that we sent.

Some people have mentioned to us that we should have "broken into the nursing home" to see my mom during this time period (she was put there by my sister shortly after her stay at my sister's home didn't work out). It turns out that there was no way we could have gotten in, because a friend of my sister's ran the front desk. We found out she had been told to call my sister the minute we entered the building.

This was all my sister's way of "protecting" our mother. Where does it say in the Bible that we are to be held back from knowing the truth? Nowhere! There is a huge difference between protecting and controlling someone!

In a final effort to try to bring peace to the situation, we signed over our half-ownership of my mother's house and went through a lawyer to give our half of the proceeds of the sale of that house to my sister to pay for anything my mother might want or need. You would think that giving away our inheritance would have at least brought about a "thank you" from my sister, but we didn't receive even that. Another symptom of false or immature Christians is never forgiving others or admitting their own wrongs and having convenient "amnesia," remembering what they want to remember and believing their own lies. Romans 1:28–31 says, *"And just as they did not see fit to acknowledge God any longer, God gave them over to a depraved mind to do those things which are not proper, being filled with all unrighteousness, wickedness, greed, evil, full of envy, murder, strife, deceit, malice, they are gossips, slanderers, haters of God insolent, arrogant, boastful, inventors of evil, disobedient to parents, without understanding, untrustworthy, unloving, unmerciful . . ."*

## Chapter 6
# False Guilt

*"There is therefore now no condemnation for those who are in Christ Jesus."* Romans 8:1

Probably the hardest part of this whole ordeal was the false guilt (as our main counselor called it) that we would experience, especially around the holidays. We knew that those were days on which we were being spoken against or cursed by the family for "not being there" with my mother, though we had been shunned by them and asked to stay away. We would actually feel those "prayers" of cursing on those days and would have to enlist intercessors to pray for us to get us through those days. We thank them and the true friends who embraced us as family on those holidays.

We found throughout this situation that there are people you just simply can never do enough for—and the more you give them, the more selfish they get. Selfishness, by the way, is not a fruit of the Spirit, and the Word says we will know true Christians by their fruit: love joy, peace, patience, kindness, goodness, faithfulness, gentleness, and self-control. We were seeing none of these fruits in my sister.

So we plodded on day by day for several years, being continually cursed and lied about.

## Chapter 7
# The Vindication

*"But the salvation of the righteous is from the Lord; He is their strength in time of trouble. The Lord helps them and delivers them; He delivers them from the wicked and saves them, because they take refuge in Him."* Psalm 37:39–40 NASB

Finally, after several years of this kind of treatment, we, in a series of strange events, were "given permission" by the family to see my mother as she neared death. So, when my husband and I went to her, we asked her many times if she could hear us and understand us. She repeatedly said "yes" and carried out a full conversation with us, without the rest of the family present. We hugged and kissed her, telling her our side of the story. Her eyes began to widen, as she said she had no idea of our side and confirmed that she had never seen any of the letters we sent her. The truth had now been spoken and she accepted it as such! She needed to hear the truth before she died. We were informed three days later (not by a family member) that she passed away. God bless her, the truth prevailed, and we believe she is in

Heaven now, where she will never be deceived or controlled again!

After my mother's death, we wondered if we should go to her funeral, but after reading the obituary my sister wrote, we knew we wouldn't even attempt it. As expected, the obituary was full of glowing reports of all my sister had done to help my mother over the years, and I was not listed as one of my mother's adult children, nor was my name or my husband's even mentioned. Luke 9:60 tells us, *"Allow the dead to bury their own dead"* (NASB). We had to let the spiritually dead ones literally go and bury their own dead. We had been completely eliminated from the family. that people with strong controlling spirits within them will either control you or eliminate you. The Lord, however, has been faithful to us, preparing us for this, and we give Him thanks.

We also felt vindicated by the large number of beautiful sympathy cards and phone calls we received, some even from a few "secret relatives"(!) telling us of their love for us. Many people stated that they "knew the truth all along" and what my sister wrote in the obituary showed them her "true colors."

Jesus said we are to forgive and pray for those who persecute us and that they "don't know what they are doing" when they are hurting us. I had never understood that verse and had asked the Lord many times about it. I thought, *How could people not know what they're doing when they are cursing and hurting you?* I recently heard a teaching about that verse that gave me a whole new perspective on it. The man who was teaching stated, "Our persecutors may know what they are doing, but they have no idea how their persecutions can lead us to a whole new place in the Lord and to his purpose being fulfilled for us." What we went through will be used to help us help others. So, in essence, they don't know that their evil deeds are for God's glory and to move us on to better things! Genesis 50:20 says, "As for you, you meant evil against me, but God meant it for good in order to bring about this present result, to preserve many people alive" (NASB). Hopefully, this writing will help many others to endure, staying strong and remaining faithful in the midst of controlling situations in their lives and ultimately bring people to Jesus.

My husband and I are now helping others in many ways we never thought we would—especially helping those who have been verbally or physically abused by their own families.

Jesus, in Luke 22:32–33, says to Simon Peter, "Satan has demanded permission to sift you like wheat, but I have prayed for you, that your faith may not fail; and you, when once you have turned again, strengthen your brothers" (NASB). My only goal in writing this story is to glorify Jesus and to help you understand how to "get to the other side" of your trial, and then I hope you will help others through their trials. (2 Corinthians 1:3–5 reminds us to comfort the afflicted with the comfort we ourselves have received from God.)

Matthew 10:34–37 says this: "Do not think that I came to bring peace on the earth; I did not come to bring peace, but a sword. For I came to set a man against his father, and a daughter against her mother, and a daughter-in-law against her mother-in-law, and a man's enemies will be the members of his household. He who loves father or mother more than Me is not worthy of Me; and he who loves son or daughter more than Me is not worthy of Me" (NASB). In essence, we must love God even more than we love our families. Matthew 19:29 states, *"And everyone who has left houses or brothers or sisters or father or mother or children or farms for My name's sake will receive many times as much, and will inherit eternal life"* (NASB).

## Chapter 8
# It's a New Day

*"For if a man is in Christ he becomes a new person altogether—the past is finished and gone, everything has become fresh and new."*

2 Corinthians 5:17 Phillips

About a month before I was "allowed" to see my mother after several years had passed, the Lord woke me one day and showed me that we were to go back to where my mom was living and wait on Him. He also said, "It's a new day."

I would like to help those in the middle of bad, controlling family situations with some words of wisdom that we were given. Some are from counselors and some were given to us by the Lord. Pray about them. Every one of them may not pertain to you but they may still be useful. Be blessed and may you be lead to your "new day."

**1. Remember to trust God**. He will vindicate you if your heart is right with Him. The vindication may take time, and sometimes you may be vindicated in heaven rather than here on earth, but God sees all!

**2. When people curse you, do not curse them back.** That only leads to your curses coming back on you, like a boomerang, through retaliating spirits. Instead, forgive. We came to a place of forgiving my sister while not agreeing with her actions. Although we were not allowed to communicate this forgiveness to her, God knew our heart. However, we do not have to trust her or keep putting ourselves back into a place of abuse. We just simply would not align ourselves with evil.

**3. Be careful who you trust.** Jesus even said He did not entrust Himself to anyone, because He knew what was in their hearts. This doesn't mean we are not to trust anybody, but we must be discerning and ask the Lord who we can trust. This is not always obvious to the human eye. Some of the people we thought we could confide in ended up betraying us, but several we thought weren't on our side surprised us with many true blessings.

**4. We learned, as the Bible says, to "turn away from" people who "cause dissensions and hindrances" (Romans 16:17).** Do not keep walking back into the lives of abusers—even if they are "family." If you get burned enough times, you will learn to avoid them! Pray "deliver us from evil," and watch the hand of the Lord help you again and again. Jesus once asked, "Who is My mother, and who are My brothers?" (Matthew 12:48 NASB). The answer isn't always our blood family; more often it is true, likeminded believers. In our case, we literally had to "let the dead bury their own dead." Put God first, before your family!

**5. Seek good, sound, godly counsellors and thank God for them.**

**6. Hold fast to any true visions or words the Lord has given you through this process.** As the saying goes, "Don't doubt in the dark what God has given you in the light!"

**7. Be able to know and discern who good-yet-evil people are.** These people call themselves Christians, but they are game players and are leading a double life. Proverbs 11:9 points out how important discernment is: "With his mouth the godless man destroys his neighbor, but through knowledge and superior discernment shall the righteous be delivered" (Amplified Bible). Here are some red flags to be aware of. Look for some of these qualities in the person. This list is taken from the book *Discernment* [3] by Charles Pretlow:

---

[3] Charles Pretlow, *Discernment,* Wilderness Voice Publishing, Canon City, CO, pp 41-42.

- Lack of empathy towards others. . . .
- A narcissistic approach in relationships—controlling and manipulative.
- Easily falling into stints of self-pity when things do not go the way they should. . . .
- Builds self up at the expense of others, often pointing out the failures of others. Has an extreme, insecure drive to constantly appear good and be correct or right, especially during arguments or disagreements.
- Often maintains a cowardly approach to life and is frequently overcome with hysteria in crisis—lacks faith and character for healthy risk taking. Lives in terror of discovery and fear of failure. . . .
- Extreme hatred and rage bottled up within but not exhibited. Usually a flat affect or expressionless look with frozen body language appears when rubbed the wrong way.
- Changes accounts of situations and events; own version is usually slanted and perceptions of what actually took place are distorted. . . . Lying to the point of believing own lies.
- Callous and often lacks conscience; unwilling to admit wrongdoing.
- Revengeful, spiteful, and mean-spirited—will conspire with others to get even.
- Often energy in life, work, sports, church work, and ministry is driven by bitter jealousy with selfish ambition that is very hard to detect. . . .

- Becomes a tireless martyr, bringing upon selves undue suffering, and in turn enlist others to feel sorry for their plight; then will use pity on others as a flattering tool to gain an advantage. (Self-pity is one of Satan's favorite human traps.) . . .
- Often imputes own hidden (unconscious), sinful motives to the behavior and actions of others; falsely accuses others.
- Gossips, slanders, and points out flaws until the victim's reputation is ruined. . . . Enlists others to aid in attacks.
- Tends to conceal true feelings and intentions of the heart; is superficial in relationships, having little or no true humility, self-disclosure, or repentance. Has a hard time admitting failures, and mistakes or errors are minimized, rationalized, and/or justified if caught red-handed.

People who are "good evil" often have the "convenient amnesia" I mentioned before—they remember what they want to remember and what's too painful to remember, they simply choose to forget! It's important to know that the "good evil" are the most dangerous and subtle people to deal with.

As the Lord leads you, pray for these people—some do actually turn around if they have not "crossed over" to the reprobate stage.

(Reprobates or those close to that stage often believe their own lies to be true.)

**8. Read your Bible daily and pray for strength in the battle.** Reading the story of Joseph as well as the Psalms may be helpful. Joseph and David both knew a little bit about being hated and chased down by evil, jealous people.

**9. Set up boundaries with any family member who is harassing you.** We had to do this after my sister banished us from the family. Write a letter stating that they are no longer allowed to phone you or to come onto your property, for instance. You may have to change your phone number and tell them the only way they can now contact you is in writing—this way you have proof of what they say, and it will not be your word against theirs. Always keep an extra copy of anything they write to you (or you to them). You may even need to have those papers filed by a lawyer or use them to file a restraining order with the police. Make sure you have caller ID on your phone and check to see who's calling before you automatically pick up. Keep in mind that when someone is verbally abusive, you do not need to give them any information about your life. They have lost the privilege of knowing those things. Keeping these people at a distance is to your advantage.

**10. Have people who are likeminded and trustworthy pray for you.** We never would have survived emotionally without our intercessors.

**11. Stay in fellowship with those who are likeminded.** Even if it's in a small home-group setting, remember, wherever two or three are gathered, He is in the midst of you.

**12. Deal with your own root issues of the heart.** Address any jealousy, lust, anger, unforgiveness, etc., to make sure you are not making the attacks on you any worse. Be honest with yourself and truly let God show you your own issues. Ask for forgiveness from the Lord (see 1 John 1:9), and ask God to help you change to reflect Him.

**13. Be alert to the possibility of being "prayed against."** If you feel any of the following symptoms, you may be being "prayed against" by your enemies, or they may be projecting their spirit onto you or cursing you. (These are called witchcraft prayers and are said by so-called Christians. A witchcraft prayer can be described as praying for one's own will with selfishness and malice in the heart.) Watch out for the following feelings, which may indicate that you are being prayed against: discouragement, spiritual heaviness and lethargy, unexplainable anxiety, powerful negative emotions, physical pain or illness, frustrating circumstances and unexplainable accidents, confusion, hopelessness, loss of will for living, etc.

If you are being prayed against, what do you do? Entire courses have been taught on this subject, but one brief suggestion would be to command the spirit off of you and also command the spirit of the person who is praying against you to leave you. It does not matter if you do not know who is praying against you—*God* knows!

**14. Do not put your relative above God and what He has told you to do in your life.** (See Luke 18:29–30.) You can still honor your relative from a distance.

**15. Be aware of how strong "groupthink" or "pack mentality" can be.** People are easily controlled by a controlling person and out of fear will do whatever they say! (And people are often threatened by the controller to get them to agree.)

**16. Move on and help others.** Don't keep your experience all to yourself (see 2 Corinthians 1:3–5).

Matthew 5 says that the persecuted will be blessed. It is often a tough battle, but the Lord will help you fight that battle. *Be blessed!*

# Prayer for Dealing with Controlling Relatives

Here is a suggested prayer to help you through this process of breaking free from controlling relatives:

Lord, I repent for allowing any unhealthy or ungodly tie to have been formed in my life, and I repent of the idolatry of getting bonded to them.

Lord, I forgive anyone for any domination, intimidation, or manipulation that they have imposed on me. I forgive them for trying to control me.

Lord, I also ask You to forgive me for yielding to that control in any way, and I also ask You to forgive me for any way that I have sought to control others through intimidation or manipulation of any sort, whether I did it knowingly or not.

I renounce any unhealthy part of those ties and I break these ties over me and my mind, will, and emotions. I rebuke any spirits of control, intimidation, conniving, or manipulation over me. I also rebuke all spirits of witchcraft and divination; I command them off of my life and body.

I pray for complete healing, Lord, so that I will be whole within my mind, will, and emotions. Make me know that I have to do my part by dealing with my own issues in my heart also. Let me hear Your voice tell me what steps to take to have a clean heart.

Make me totally free in You, Jesus, and help me to remember to purposely bind myself to godly people from now on and give me the strength I need to do that.

Amen.

www.ingramcontent.com/pod-product-compliance
Lightning Source LLC
Chambersburg PA
CBHW020025050426
42450CB00005B/642